Entrepreneurs

Krista McLuskey

Crabtree Publishing Company

Dedication

This series is dedicated to every woman who has followed her dreams and to every young girl who hopes to do the same. While overcoming great odds and often oppression, the remarkable women in this series have triumphed in their fields. Their dedication, hard work, and excellence can serve as an inspiration to all—young and old, male and female. Women in Profile is both an acknowledgment of and a tribute to these great women.

Project Coordinator
Leslie Strudwick
Crabtree Editor
Virginia Mainprize
Editing and Proofreading
Carlotta Lemieux
Alana Luft
Design
Warren Clark

Published by Crabtree Publishing Company

350 Fifth Avenue, Suite 3308
New York, NY
USA 10018

360 York Road, R.R. 4
Niagara-on-the-Lake
Ontario, Canada
L0S 1J0

Cataloging-in-Publication Data

McLuskey, Krista, 1974–
      Entrepreneurs / Krista McLuskey.
           p. cm. — (Women in profile)
      Includes bibliographical references and index.
      Summary: Chronicles the lives and groundbreaking achievements of women in business, including fashion designer Coco Chanel, film studio head Mary Pickford, and Body Shop founder Anita Roddick.
      ISBN 0-7787-0034-8 (pbk.). — ISBN 0-7787-0012-7-RLB
      1. Women executives—Biography—Juvenile literature. 2. Businesswomen—Biography—Juvenile literature. 3. Women-owned business enterprises—Juvenile literature. 4. Entrepreneurship—Juvenile literature. [1. Businesswomen. 2. Women-Biography.]
I. Title II. Series.
HD6054.3.M4   1999
338'.04'0820922-dc21
[B]   98-37123
                                                 CIP
                                               AC

Photograph Credits

Every reasonable effort has been made to trace ownership and to obtain permission to reprint copyright material. The publishers would be pleased to have any errors or omissions brought to their attention so that they may be corrected in subsequent printings.

Archive Photos: cover, pages 6, 12, 18, 27, 36; Courtesy of The Body Shop, UK: pages 20, 22 (Carol Beckwith), 19, 21, 23; Canapress Photo Service: pages 17, 26, 29, 41; Corbis-Bettmann: page 15; Courtesy of Gentl & Hyers: page 24; Image Works: page 7; Krista McLuskey: page 10; Courtesy of Jean Nidetch: page 43; Photofest: pages 13, 14, 37, 38, 39, 40; Courtesy of Shahnaz Herbals: page 42; Courtesy of Randee St. Nicholas: pages 25, 28; Courtesy of Jannie Tay/The Hour Glass: pages 30, 31, 32, 33, 34, 35; Topham/Image Works: pages 9, 16; UPI/Corbis-Bettmann: pages 8, 11, 44, 45.

Contents

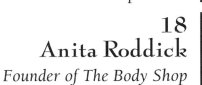

Entrepreneurs

Entrepreneurs are people who organize and manage businesses. They hope to make a profit but are aware that they risk losing money. Entrepreneurs need imagination to create an original idea, to plan how to get the money to start their business, and to convince people to buy their product. They also need courage. An entrepreneur often has created a product that no one has seen or used, and does not know if people will even be interested in the product.

Women entrepreneurs need even more courage and imagination than men because business traditionally has been considered a "man's world." To be taken seriously in the business world, women entrepreneurs have to convince men that women can be successful business people. They have to overcome the prejudices of those who do not respect women as co-workers, bosses, or **competitors**.

The number of women entrepreneurs is growing every year. Women are starting their own businesses at twice the rate of men, but they are still a minority in the business world.

The women entrepreneurs in this book come from many different backgrounds. Some were wealthy and used their wealth to create more money. Some began with no money and made fortunes from a combination of a good idea and their determination. Some were housewives who wanted more than a traditional female role. All these women used their different skills to create a place for themselves in the business world.

Although the women in this book met obstacles on the road to success, they all became respected entrepreneurs. Their stories are an inspiration for anyone with a desire to achieve.

"Fashion is not something that exists in dresses only; fashion is something in the air. It's the wind that blows in the new fashion; you feel it coming, you smell it. Fashion is in the sky, in the street, fashion has to do with ideas, the way we live, what is happening."

Gabrielle "Coco" Chanel

Founder of the House of Chanel

Early Years

Coco was born in Samur, France. When Coco was eleven, her mother died, and the family was split up. Coco's father was a merchant who traveled from town to town selling goods. Without his wife to help him, he could not look after the children. He sent his sons to a farm, where they worked as laborers. Coco and her two sisters were sent to an orphanage. Coco never saw her father again.

Coco was miserable at the orphanage. The nuns who ran it were very strict. When Coco was eighteen, she and her older sister were sent to a girls boarding school, but that was not much better. Most of the girls came from wealthy homes, and they were unkind to the few who were from the orphanage.

Happily for Coco, one girl was kind. She was a relative, and she took Coco and her sister to see their aunt, Louise Costier. Louise was a **seamstress**, who had a talent for making old dresses look new and fashionable. Watching her, Coco realized that sewing could be fun, if you used your imagination.

Backgrounder

Orphanages

Orphanages are places that house children whose parents have died or cannot look after them. Many orphanages used to be run by religious people. They took the children into their care, taught them religion, and educated them. Most orphanages in Europe and North America have closed over the years. Childcare experts now prefer to place children in foster care (a child being taken in and looked after by a family) or group homes (a small number of children being looked after by trained childcare workers) so children receive more individual attention from the adults looking after them.

Coco learned to sew at the orphanage, but it was her aunt who taught her to enjoy creating fashionable clothes.

Developing Skills

Coco took several jobs in clothing shops before deciding to try a career in singing. This attempt was short and unsuccessful.

Coco dressed and acted rebelliously for her time, wearing plain, comfortable clothes and riding **astride** a horse. Other women dressed in much fancier clothing and rode sidesaddle.

Coco began making hats for some of her wealthy friends. In those days, fashionable women wore huge hats, covered with frills and feathers. Coco's hats were simple and practical, and they were so popular that in 1910 she hired a professional hat maker to help her. She opened a little shop in a friend's apartment. Soon, she moved to a larger shop with money she borrowed from another friend, Arthur Capel. Coco wanted to be very independent, so when Arthur gave her money for her next two shops, she promised to repay it.

Once Coco left the orphanage, she worked hard to escape from her unhappy life.

In 1913, Coco began making clothes as well as hats. Her clothing **designs** were very simple, without any frills or lace. Her clothes became fashionable among the French **nobility**. That same year, Coco opened a shop in the coastal town of Deauville. Because people came to Deauville to relax and take part in sports, Coco's loose-fitting designs were a big hit.

Coco was in Deauville when World War I broke out. Many of the town's hotels were converted into hospitals for wounded soldiers. Coco adapted to the new situation and began making straight dresses and little hats for the nurses.

During the war, French women began to work outside the home, doing jobs that soldiers had left vacant. Coco's shop did excellent business because she realized that women would need looser clothing in which to work. Her designs fitted the needs of this new lifestyle.

The success of these new designs convinced Coco and Arthur to open a "maison de couture," a fashion house, in the fashionable seaside town of Biarritz. This shop was by far her biggest yet. Coco was thirty-two years old. Her fashion house did so well that Coco repaid Arthur all the money he had lent her over the years.

BACKGROUNDER

Money to Spend

When men went off to fight in World War I (1914–1918), many jobs were left vacant. Women began to take over these jobs to keep the businesses going during the war. This was the first time that many of these women had money of their own to spend. Before, they had had to ask their husbands or fathers for money. Women liked being able to buy whatever they wanted and needed. When the men came back from the war, working women were told it was their duty to give the jobs back to the men.

"Nothing makes a woman look older than obvious expensiveness, ornateness, complication. I still dress as I always did, like a schoolgirl."

Accomplishments

In 1919, Arthur was killed in a car crash. To try to forget her sadness and loneliness, Coco worked harder than ever. She decided to try something new and create her first perfume. Perfumes at that time all smelled of natural scents, such as roses and other flowers. Coco wanted to produce a perfume that did not imitate other scents, one that would make women smell unique. She hired a "master nose," a person who made perfume. He mixed up ten samples from which she could choose, and she picked the fifth sample. That is why she named it Chanel No. 5.

Coco packaged Chanel No. 5 in the same style as her clothes. It was put in plain, colorless bottles, unlike most perfume of the day, which was in fancy, colored bottles. The perfume sold exceptionally well and is still on the market.

The late 1920s were the peak of Coco's success. Business was booming and her designs were the leading fashion. In 1936, her life took a down turn when her employees staged a strike. After a long battle, Coco had to give in to their demands for holiday pay and higher wages. She never recovered from this defeat, and she began to distrust her workers. In 1939, Coco laid off most of her employees and closed the House of Chanel. The only business she continued was her perfume company, which was still very successful.

Coco had an excellent sense of smell. She said that when people gave her a flower, she could smell the scent of their hand on the stem.

Throughout the 1940s and 1950s, most of Coco's best friends died. She lived an isolated life seeing few people. Her wealth continued to grow because of the sales of Chanel No. 5, and by the time she was sixty-five, she was one of the richest women in the world.

In 1954, Coco came out of retirement. She was angry that most of the new designers were men and that they were not designing practical clothes. Women ought to be able to get into a car "without splitting their seams," she said. "Clothes should have a natural shape!"

As before, the clothes Coco designed were simple and comfortable. The critics disliked her first show, but her second show was a different story. The fashion world loved it. Coco continued designing clothes for seventeen more years. She was lonely without her friends but kept herself busy with her work.

At the age of eighty-eight, Coco lay down on her bed, fully dressed, and died with only her maid at her side. The last collection she had designed was shown later that month. Her clothing designs are still popular today.

Quick Notes

- In 1922, Coco made suntans popular. Before then, women had tried to keep their skin as fair as possible to show that they did not work outdoors like farmers and other laborers.

- Instead of wearing her expensive jewelry on a day-to-day basis, Coco wore a lot of fake jewelry. She started the trend of wearing costume jewelry.

- It was during her brief singing career that Coco got her nickname. Two songs she often sang were "Ko Ko Ri Ko" and "Qui qu'a vu Coco dans la Trocadéro?" which means "Who has seen Coco (a dog) in the Trocadéro (a section of Paris)?"

"She will certainly go down in history as the only couturier who spanned the taste of almost half a century without ever changing her basic concept of clothes."

Bettina Ballard, fashion editor at *Vogue* magazine

"I've worked and fought my way through since I was twelve, and I know business."

Mary Pickford

Cofounder of United Artists Corporation

Early Years

Mary was born the same year the first movie was made, the very thing that would bring her such fame. She was born in Toronto, Canada.

When Mary was four years old, her father died, leaving her mother, Charlotte, to support three children. Charlotte took on several jobs, including sewing and playing small roles in a local theater company, but she struggled to support her family. Neighbors often brought them meals to keep them from going hungry.

Charlotte decided to let Mary try acting to help bring in some extra money. Mary acted in her first play at the age of five, in a part that had only one line. When the next play came along, it was suggested that Mary take a larger role. Her mother did not think Mary would be able to learn so many lines, but Mary said, "I can do it!" The next day, Mary knew every one of her lines.

Mary loved acting on stage. She loved the feeling of excitement as the curtain went up and the audience grew silent. The audiences loved Mary. Her golden curls, her dimples, and her innocent manner caught people's attention.

BACKGROUNDER

Kinetoscope

Thomas Edison, the inventor of the light bulb, wanted to make a machine that would make pictures appear to move. In 1888, he began experimenting but set aside the project without success. He had his assistant, William Kennedy Laurie Dickson, continue trying to create moving pictures. In 1893, Dickson succeeded with a machine called the Kinetoscope and made the world's first movie. It was called *Record of a Sneeze*. It showed the different movements of a man sneezing. *Record of a Sneeze* was shown for the first time in 1894, in New York City.

Mary's real name was Gladys Mary Smith.

At the beginning of her film career, Mary was known to her film audiences as "The Biograph Girl with the Curls." She was not listed in the film credits at the end of the movie as actors' names are today.

Developing Skills

When Mary was eight years old, her mother joined a traveling theater company and took the family with her. Mary was given parts in many of the plays. Life on the road was not easy for such a young girl. She had to catch trains in the middle of the night, and she rarely stayed in the same town for more than a day.

At the age of fourteen, Mary and her family were on tour with a play in New York City. She wanted to act in a Broadway play and decided to audition for a role in *The Warrens of Virginia*. She got a part as a young child. When her family went back to Toronto, Mary stayed in New York City. People were charmed by Mary's sincere style of acting.

While she was in New York, Mary saw her first movie. She realized that acting in films was a way she could earn more money for her family. She went to the Biograph Motion Picture Company, but she was offered less money than she had been making on the stage. Mary put her foot down, insisting she would not work for so little. The film studio director D.W. Griffith agreed to her demands, and Mary became a regular actress at Biograph. Within three months, she was getting rave reviews in the newspapers.

Between 1909 and 1911, Mary made eighty-one silent films for Biograph, working each day from 9 A.M. until 8 P.M. She became America's greatest film star. She was known as "America's Sweetheart" because of the innocent and cute characters she played. By 1919, now working for Famous Players, another Hollywood film studio, Mary was making a huge amount of money for the time—$4,000 a week! People flocked to see a film just because she was in it. Later that year, she **negotiated** a salary of $10,000 a week.

Mary was no longer famous only as an actress. She was now a businesswoman with whom Hollywood producers had to reckon. She knew how much her acting was worth to the film studios, and when negotiating her wages, she held out for as much as she could get.

"I decided that if I was to be a success by the time I was twenty, I had best be stirring … when I saw the things other girls had, I was determined to have them, but I would not get them from my family; I'd work for them."

During World War I, Mary spoke at rallies, encouraging people to support the war effort.

Quick Notes

- Because Mary was away acting during most of her childhood, she had only a few months of schooling in her whole life. Even so, she taught herself to read.

- During World War I, Mary often went to an army base in San Diego, California, and gave each soldier a gold locket with her picture in it. She was made an honorary colonel, and the battalion was nicknamed "Mary Pickford's Fighting 600."

- In 1925, some people tried to kidnap Mary. Police had been alerted ahead of time so the kidnappers were caught and put in jail. For some time after that, Mary was guarded twenty-four hours a day.

Accomplishments

Mary was still not happy with her salary. She knew that she was making Famous Players a lot of money, and she thought she deserved more of that money. She also wanted more creative control of the content and presentation of the films in which she appeared. To get this control, Mary decided to form her own company, together with two other film stars, Douglas Fairbanks and the comedian Charlie Chaplin. Mary, Douglas, and Charlie were the most famous film stars of the era, so they knew that people would come to watch their movies, even if they were not made by a well-known production company. D.W. Griffith, Mary's director at Biograph, who had become extremely successful, was a fourth partner.

"We maniacs had fun and made good pictures and a lot of money. We produced and financed our own pictures, and if they lost money— which they never did—we were prepared to accept the losses as well as the profits."

The signing of the contract for United Artists. The founding members included Douglas Fairbanks (left), Charlie Chaplin (second from the left), Mary Pickford (right), and D.W. Griffith (sitting).

In 1919, the four film artists, led by Mary, formed United Artists Corporation. United Artists was the first film production company to be controlled by artists, not business executives. This was a big risk, but Mary was confident they would succeed. With complete creative control over their work, the group made some of the best films of their lives and were able to keep the profits for themselves.

From this point on, Mary was considered one of the shrewdest business people in Hollywood. She had founded a company that changed how Hollywood films were produced. Mary's insistence on perfection in the United Artists' films improved the whole movie industry, and set a high standard that other companies tried to follow.

Douglas Fairbanks and Mary were married in 1920. They became known as the "king and queen of Hollywood." United Artists continued to prosper, switching to talking movies in the late 1920s. Douglas Fairbanks, Mary, and many other famous Hollywood figures formed the Academy of Motion Picture Arts and Sciences in 1927. Two years later, Mary won an Academy Award for her first role in a talking picture, *Coquette*.

In 1932, Mary retired from acting to take up a career as a writer. She remained involved in Hollywood film production for many years, but her most important accomplishment remained her role in forming the United Artists Corporation.

BACKGROUNDER

Academy of Motion Picture Arts and Sciences

Founded in 1927, the Academy of Motion Picture Arts and Sciences is an organization of people from all aspects of the film-making industry, including scriptwriters, directors, actors, and producers. It is a non-profit organization, and its goal is to improve both the art and science of films. Each year, it honors the best people in all areas of film-making by presenting the Academy Awards. These awards, nicknamed the Oscars, are highly **coveted** by people in the film industry. Actors winning an Oscar often get better roles. Films often get more viewers and make more money.

* * * * * * * * * * * * * * * *

In 1976, at the age of eighty-three, Mary was presented with an honorary Academy Award in recognition of her great contribution to the film industry.

*"To succeed you have to
believe in something
with such a passion that
it becomes reality."*

Anita Roddick

Founder of The Body Shop

Early Years

A nita was born in Littlehampton, England, where her parents owned the Clifton Café. When Anita was eight years old, her parents divorced, and her mother remarried. Anita's new father, Henry, turned the Clifton Café into an American-style diner like the ones he had seen while living in the United States. It was complete with pinball machines, a juke box, and Coca-Cola, which was not well known in England at that time. Suddenly, the café became very popular. Anita realized that the atmosphere in a business can make it successful.

When Anita was about ten years old, Henry died, and her mother took over the café. All the children were expected to work there after school and on weekends to help support the family. Meanwhile, Anita was completing her education. After finishing secondary school, she attended a teacher training college in the city of Bath.

BACKGROUNDER

Littlehampton's Italian Community

Littlehampton is a small seaside town in the south of England. Several Italian families lived there when Anita was a child. Most of the families were related to her. Anita's parents, Gilda and Donny Perella, and her stepfather, Henry, were all born in Atina, a village in central Italy.

Anita on Littlehampton beach.

Developing Skills

After graduating, Anita decided she wanted some adventure in her life. She traveled to Tahiti, New Hebrides, Australia, Madagascar, New Caledonia, and South Africa. In these places, Anita watched the local women use natural products to clean their skin and hair. She tried them and found they worked better than the products she used back in England.

After Anita returned to England, she met and married Gordon Roddick, with whom she had two daughters. Anita and Gordon worked hard running a hotel and restaurant. One day, Gordon announced that he wanted to take two years off to ride on horseback from Buenos Aires, Argentina, to New York City. Although Anita was not thrilled at this prospect, she knew that it was his dream. She had to plan how to support herself and the children while Gordon was away. She decided to run a little shop that would be open only from 9 A.M. to 5 P.M. so that she could spend time with her daughters.

Anita decided that it would be a **cosmetics** shop selling products made from only natural ingredients. During her travels, she had seen how effective natural products were. She had noticed that women in those hot countries had silky smooth skin even though they were in the sun all the time.

"It was a revelation to realize that there were women all over the world caring for their bodies perfectly well without ever buying a single cosmetic."

After getting a £4,000 bank loan, Anita hired a chemist to develop the cosmetics. She told the chemist not to test the products on animals, even though that is normal practice in the cosmetics industry. Anita rented a store in Brighton, 20 miles (33 kilometers) from Littlehampton. She painted the inside dark green to hide stains on the walls. In March 1976, the first Body Shop opened, and it made £130 the first day.

Anita had only twenty-five products to sell. To fill the space in the shop she packaged each product in five different sizes. She bought the cheapest containers she could find. Since she could not afford very many bottles, she asked customers to bring in their own to fill them in the store. In this way, Anita began recycling before it was commonly done.

Anita used unusual marketing tactics. To get customers into The Body Shop, she sprayed a trail of perfume down the street leading to the store to tempt people to come inside. She hung dried flowers from the ceiling and put bowls of scented **potpourri** on the counters.

Quick Notes

- Anita uses her company delivery trucks as mobile billboards. Written on the side of each one are slogans such as, "If you think education is expensive, try ignorance."

- Anita was named London's Business Woman of the Year in 1986.

- Anita came up with the name of her company from signs she had seen at garages in the United States—body shops.

"If you have a company with itsy-bitsy vision you have an itsy-bitsy company."

Bottling products was a time-consuming job at The Body Shop.

Accomplishments

Within a year, Anita decided to open a second Body Shop in a nearby town. The bank refused to lend her any more money, so she teamed up with a partner who paid to set up the shop in return for half of the business. Gordon, her husband, returned from his travels and began to help by bottling the products and taking care of the finances.

Soon, people came to Anita wanting to open their own Body Shop stores with products supplied by her. Anita and Gordon agreed because this was a way of expanding the business. The first Body Shop **franchises** opened in 1978, one in England and one in Brussels, Belgium. Anita and Gordon always trained the new Body Shop owners, teaching them about skin and hair care, and about all the ingredients in the products.

"For us it could never be morally acceptable to abuse an animal for something so trivial as face cream."

During the next few years, the number of stores and franchises increased. Meanwhile, Anita invented new products whenever she saw a need. She created a peppermint lotion to soothe sore feet after several people, who had run a race, came into the store asking for foot lotion.

Anita traveled the world looking for natural ingredients that were used by other cultures for body care.

In 1984, Anita and Gordon decided to sell Body Shop shares on the stock market. By this time, they had thirty-eight shops in England and fifty-two shops in other countries. So many shares sold the first day on the stock market that overnight Anita and Gordon were millionaires.

Anita began thinking about the social responsibility business had. She wanted to help her community and the environment. She began by sponsoring posters for **Greenpeace**, which was trying to prevent hazardous waste from being dumped in the ocean. Next, she campaigned against the overhunting of whales. She put up posters in her shops and stickers on her bottles saying "Save the whales." She also supported recycling and efforts to preserve the rain forest. Body Shop delivery trucks became billboards for Anita's various causes. Her campaigns focused on human rights and environmental issues, such as protecting endangered species.

Anita's business continues to grow. Today, The Body Shop has approximately 1,500 stores in forty-six countries.

BACKGROUNDER
Stock Market

Stock is the financial worth of a company divided into equal sections, called shares. One person can own all the stock in a company. If a company needs extra money to expand its business, it sometimes sells its stock to the public. Shares are sold to the public on the stock market, which is the place where people buy and sell shares in companies. When stock in a company is sold like this, many people own small parts of the company, and the profits are divided among the owners of these shares. The original owners lose some control because they have to answer to their shareholders if the company does not make a profit.

"Along with the profit and loss sheets, I would want to know about the profit and loss for the environment, or the community or the Third World"

Anita with her husband and two daughters.

"Create something that you love in your lifetime. Not only work, but pleasurable things like gardening got me through a lot of hard times."

Martha Stewart

Founder of Martha Stewart Living Omnimedia

Early Years

Martha planted her first seeds in her backyard in Nutley, New Jersey, when she was only three years old. Her father, a keen gardener, showed her how to grow vegetables and flowers. Soon, gardening became one of her favorite hobbies.

Another hobby was cooking, which she learned from her mother. Martha had five brothers and sisters, so she had plenty of practice cooking and baking for them.

Learning was fun for Martha, and she did very well in school. She won a partial scholarship to college and worked as a model to pay for the rest of her school expenses. While still at Barnard College in New York City, Martha married Andy Stewart. She graduated in 1963 and continued modeling in television commercials.

BACKGROUNDER

Martha's Parents

Martha's parents, Edward and Martha Kostyra, were of Polish origin. They taught their children that they could achieve anything in life if they worked hard enough. From a young age, the children were encouraged to do things for themselves, such as painting their own rooms and sewing their own clothes.

Martha has always been an animal lover.

Developing Skills

In 1967, Martha got a job as a stockbroker, buying and selling shares of companies for other people. Martha was very good at her job, but she decided to quit in 1973 when business in the stock market slowed down because of a **recession**.

Martha and Andy moved to Connecticut with their daughter, Alexis. They began to restore a farmhouse that had been built in 1805. Making such an old building livable was a big challenge for Martha, but she found that she loved the experience and was very good at it.

Martha decided to use her talent for cooking and opened a catering business in 1976. For ten years, from the basement of her home, she cooked meals for people who were having large parties. The business grew into a million dollar a year operation.

Martha believes there is a correct way to do everything from planting a tree to plastering a wall, and that anyone who wants to can learn.

"I know and do the things I teach others about ... I take the simple things of life and teach others how to do them, everyday things."

During this period, Martha was also busy as a writer. She wrote articles on food and entertaining for *The New York Times* and edited and wrote columns for *House Beautiful* magazine. In 1982, Martha decided to write a book on how to entertain guests at parties and other social events. She co-authored a book called *Entertaining*. The book was filled with many color photos. It was a huge success, selling more than a million copies and making Martha famous.

Martha realized that there was a market for her skills in teaching people how to cook, display food, and decorate. She began making "how-to" videos, appearing on television specials, and writing books on cooking, restoring old homes, and gardening. She was fast becoming America's top authority on taste and decoration.

Martha's many books are beautifully designed, well written, and filled with color photographs.

BACKGROUNDER
Cross-Media Marketing

Martha's company, Martha Stewart Living Omnimedia, uses the various forms of media that it owns to promote other parts of the business. For example, *Martha Stewart Living* magazine runs advertisements for the *Martha Stewart Living* television show. The television show uses recipes from the magazine and products from *Martha by Mail*, her mail order company. In this way, people who might not buy her magazine are exposed to what it offers when they watch television or listen to her radio program. People who would not normally buy her products in a store can see them in the magazine or on television. In April 1998, Martha Stewart won an award from the American Marketing Association given to business executives who have made a significant and lasting contribution to marketing.

Martha has made a career of doing what she loves best—gardening, cooking, and decorating.

Accomplishments

In 1991, Martha signed a contract with the publishing house Time Warner to publish a magazine called *Martha Stewart Living*. The magazine was filled with gardening and decorating suggestions, recipes for all occasions, tips for entertaining, and ideas for unique make-at-home gifts. It grew from a circulation of 250,000 to more than two million copies per issue.

In 1993, Martha started a television show, also called *Martha Stewart Living*, which continued the idea of the magazine. At the beginning, the show ran once a week for half an hour. It became so popular that it was soon running six times a week and was watched by five million people. The television show has won three Emmy Awards, which recognize outstanding television programs.

In 1995, Martha expanded her business even further by publishing a mail-order catalog, called *Martha by Mail*. Its products included cake-decorating and soap-making kits, cookie cutters, and posters. That same year, Martha began to write a *New York Times* column called "Ask Martha." Readers could write in with questions about home and garden issues. The column now appears in more than two hundred newspapers in Canada and the United States. The success of Martha's column encouraged her to begin a call-in radio show, also called *Ask Martha*.

In 1997, Martha decided to buy control of the business from Time Warner. She called it Martha Stewart Living Omnimedia. Now that Martha owns her television show, radio show, magazine, and product line, she has complete control over how fast and in what ways she expands her business. It has grown rapidly in three areas: **merchandising**, publishing, and television. Martha is so busy that, as she puts it, the only thing she lacks "is the time to do all that I love to do."

Martha with her line of bed and bath products.

Quick Notes

- **Martha has six fax numbers and seven car-phone numbers.**

- **Martha was named one of "America's 25 Most Influential People" by *Time* magazine in 1996.**

- **Martha is a pet lover. She has four Chow-Chow dogs and six Himalayan cats.**

- **Martha has a line of bed and bath products that she sells at K-mart. She is also planning to sell a line of plants in K-mart garden centers.**

- **Martha's twenty-second book, *Great Parties*, was released in November 1997.**

"Women will be the leading entrepreneurs of the future because we're more flexible; we're used to balancing roles. We're willing to share, we're willing to care."

Jannie Tay

Founder of The Hour Glass Limited

Early Years

Jannie was born in the town of Ipoh in western Malaysia. She was the oldest child in a family of six children. Jannie often went on business trips around Malaysia with her father, who had a reputation as a successful and honest businessman. During these trips, she discovered that an important part of business is developing the trust of one's clients.

In Malaysia at that time, girls were not encouraged to go to university, but Jannie's father wanted her to get the best education possible. When she was sixteen years old, he sent her to school in Australia.

While Jannie was in Australia, her father died. Being the oldest child, she felt responsible for her younger brothers and sisters. She brought them all to Australia and arranged that they too got a good education. She took on the role of being both mother and father to them.

BACKGROUNDER

Malaysia

Malaysia, in Southeast Asia, became an independent country in 1963. The country is divided by the South China Sea. The capital city, Kuala Lumpur, is on the Malay Peninsula. Sarawak and Sabah are on the island of Borneo, about 400 miles (644 kilometers) away from the southern Malay Peninsula. Malaysia's two main ethnic groups are Malay and Chinese. Most Malaysians practice the Islamic religion.

Jannie (center) with her sisters (left) and her cousins (right).

Developing Skills

I n Australia, Jannie studied at Monash University, where she earned a bachelor's degree in **physiology** and a master's degree in **pharmacology**. During this time, she met Henry Chwan Tay, a medical student from Singapore. They were married in 1971 and moved to Singapore so that Henry could help run his family's watch business, Lee Chay & Co.

Jannie's first daughter, Michelle, was born that year. Michelle had **cerebral palsy** and could not see, hear, or even sit. Jannie hired a full-time nurse to look after her.

For the next few years, Jannie lectured in the physiology department at the National University of Singapore while Henry helped run the family business. When Henry decided that he would like to work as a doctor, Jannie quit her job at the university to take over his position in Lee Chay & Co. She knew nothing about business but decided to give it a try. She started as a sales clerk so she could learn all about the company. Meanwhile, she gave birth to a second daughter Audrey.

"I always see myself as a mother first. I have never seen myself as a businesswoman…. Also, I cannot say that I am ambitious. However, whatever I do, I want to do my best."

Although she was educated in the sciences, Jannie is also brilliant in the business world.

While working for Lee Chay & Co., Jannie found that the business was not doing very well. She realized that to make more money, the company should be selling top-quality watches to wealthy people. The company would never earn a good reputation if it continued selling inexpensive, poor-quality watches.

Henry's family did not agree, so Jannie and Henry decided to open their own branch of the company in 1975, the same year their son Michael was born. Their new company, Orchard Watch Pte. Ltd., sold some of the most expensive watches in the world, such as Rolex and Cartier. The new shop was in a tourist area, and the business flourished.

"When I look back at the drive that I had at the time, it was probably because I wanted to forget the hurt that I kept myself so busy. I was running around looking for help for my youngest daughter as well as keeping up with my business."

Jannie and Henry Chwan Tay were married in 1971.

Quick Notes

- Jannie is currently president of the Asean (Association of Southeast Asian Nations) Business Forum which promotes trade and economic cooperation within Southeast Asia.

- Jannie and two other Singaporean businesses jointly raised funds for the Cannossian School for the Hearing Impaired to support the training of more teachers. When she looked into education for the deaf in Singapore, Jannie found the student-to-teacher ratio was fifty-five to one.

Accomplishments

I n 1979, Jannie started a watch **retailing** company called The Hour Glass. Six months later, her daughter Michelle died. Soon afterwards, her youngest daughter, Sabrina, was born without ears, with a **cleft palate**, and with a hole in her heart. The next few years were difficult for Jannie. Sabrina had to undergo a number of major operations. She had a successful heart operation and her cleft palate was repaired. She was also fitted with a hearing aid.

Jannie continued to work very hard at The Hour Glass. She had to decide how to expand the company. She opened more stores in Singapore and also in Malaysia. Often, Jannie worked seven days a week, twelve hours a day.

Jannie and her daughter Sabrina.

In 1988, The Hour Glass began to sell shares in the company on the Singapore Stock Exchange. This brought in extra money and allowed Jannie to expand her business even more. In 1994, The Hour Glass bought control of several famous Swiss watch-making companies, giving The Hour Glass the **exclusive** right to sell these popular watches. Jannie believes that carrying high-quality watches is what makes her business so successful. She sees them as **heirlooms** and investments rather than just pieces of jewelry.

The Hour Glass opened shops selling Swiss watches in Australia, Malaysia, Hong Kong, Thailand, and Indonesia. It also began to make its own watches. The Hour Glass was growing at an incredible rate.

The company won many awards in the 1990s, and Jannie received personal recognition for her success as a businesswoman. In 1997, she was named one of the fifty leading women entrepreneurs of the world by the National Foundation for Women Business Owners. She was also named the twenty-fifth Most Powerful Woman in the World by *Marie Claire* magazine.

Despite Jannie's personal and business success, she has always felt that she owes a debt to her community. She has founded many organizations that support and encourage women entrepreneurs. She also runs charities that support schools for the hearing impaired.

"By allowing time for myself, I am able to balance my life, come back to work with renewed energy levels, ready to face whatever comes. This could save my sanity during bad times ... that may break most people."

BACKGROUNDER

National Foundation for Women Business Owners (NFWBO)

NFWBO is a non-profit organization that researches women who own businesses worldwide and shares this information with other business-women. NFWBO feels that this information will help business-women by letting them know what challenges they will face and where they can go for support. In 1997, NFWBO created a list of the fifty Leading Women Entrepreneurs of the World. Jannie Tay was one of the fifty women chosen.

Jannie has traveled the world with her business. Here she is in India in 1990.

"I don't think of myself as a poor deprived ghetto girl who made good. I think of myself as somebody who from an early age knew I was responsible for myself, and I had to make good."

Oprah Winfrey

Founder of Harpo Productions

Early Years

O prah was born in Kosciusko, Mississippi. Her mother, Vernita, did not have enough money or time to look after a baby, so Oprah was sent to live with her grandmother.

Oprah was a strong-willed little girl. By the time she was six years old, she was proving too much for her grandmother to look after. Oprah went to live with her mother who was a maid in Milwaukee, but Vernita was too busy to have much time for Oprah. To get her mother's attention, Oprah made up stories, ran away, and even faked a burglary at their house.

When Oprah was fourteen, she moved in with her father, Vernon, and her stepmother in Nashville, Tennessee. Vernon's high expectations of Oprah stopped her rebellion. She did well at school and starting acting in a drama club.

"If I hadn't been sent to my father, I would have gone in another direction. I could have made a good criminal. I would have used these same instincts differently."

BACKGROUNDER

A Young Performer

As a child, Oprah was taken to church regularly. By the time she was eight years old, she was appearing in Easter and Christmas programs at her church. She became a frequent performer at church functions because she was so good at reciting and reading. Oprah put great emotion into the words she was speaking.

Oprah began her career in television at the age of nineteen.

Developing Skills

I n 1971, Oprah got a part-time job reading the news at a local radio station. She was only seventeen years old. She also began studying at Tennessee State University, majoring in English. Her studies were financed in part by a scholarship she won for a speech she gave called "The Negro, the Constitution, and the United States."

Still in university, Oprah was hired by WTVF-TV in Nashville as a **news anchor**. She earned over $10,000 a year. She began to look for work outside Nashville, and in 1976, she found a job as a news anchor in Baltimore, Maryland. She left university only a few months before her graduation to begin this job.

"I said to myself, 'This (hosting a talk-show) is what I should be doing. It's like breathing.'"

Oprah found it impossible to keep her opinions out of the news broadcasts, and she was fired. Because of her contract with the television station she was asked to co-host a talk show, called *People Are Talking*. Here, Oprah discovered what her talents were and what she most wanted to do. Her honest approach, her ability to get on with people, and her outgoing personality made her popular with the audiences. The ratings of the show soared. The qualities that had caused Oprah to be fired from her previous job were the very ones that made her a success in this one.

In 1984, Oprah was asked to host the morning talk show *A.M. Chicago,* which was aired at the same time as the famous *Phil Donahue Show.* Before Oprah began hosting *A.M. Chicago,* the show's ratings were low. She quickly turned it into a hit, drawing viewers away from the *Phil Donahue Show.* Oprah was successful because she asked questions that other talk show hosts did not dare ask. Oprah's spunk captivated the television audiences.

Oprah decided to try acting in 1985. She played the part of Sophia in the movie *The Color Purple,* taking a leave of absence from her talk show. The critics loved Oprah in this role, and she was nominated for an Academy Award for best supporting actress. She did not win the award, but many more people became aware of her talents.

BACKGROUNDER
Appearance

While she was working on the talk show *People Are Talking,* the executives at the television station wanted Oprah to change her appearance. They said that her nose was too big, her chin was too long, and her eyes were too far apart. Because Oprah could not change any of these things, she decided to change her hairstyle, and she got a perm. The perm was a disaster, and Oprah went bald temporarily. After this experience, she vowed she would never again change her appearance to please anyone but herself.

Oprah in The Color Purple.

BACKGROUNDER

Cabrini-Green

Charitable projects have always been important to Oprah. One of the most important is a program in which she acts as a positive role model for teenage girls. She spends time with girls from a Chicago neighborhood, the Cabrini-Green housing projects. She takes the girls out for dinner, shopping, and to movies. Oprah's rule for teenagers joining this "girls' club" is that they must promise to stay in school and not get pregnant until they are older.

Accomplishments

In 1986, *A.M. Chicago* was renamed *The Oprah Winfrey Show*. It was lengthened from thirty minutes to a full hour. Within five months, *The Oprah Winfrey Show* had become the third-highest-rated television show, and the highest-rated talk show, with over nine million viewers each day. Before long, more than seventeen million viewers were tuning in each morning to watch her. Oprah became the highest-paid performer in the entertainment business, earning $30 million in 1987–1988. She was working up to fourteen hours a day.

The Oprah Winfrey Show interviews people who are experts in their field or who have been exposed to difficult issues, such as suicide, divorce, and racism. Oprah talks with her guests, often breaking into tears or bursting into laughter as she listens to the stories they tell. Oprah has shared with her television audience many of the difficult things she had to deal with in her own life. She wants her show to give hope and courage to people.

The Oprah Winfrey Show *was the number one talk show for twelve consecutive seasons.*

In 1986, Oprah founded her own company, Harpo Productions, to respond to her fan mail and create publicity for her talk show. In 1988, Harpo Productions bought *The Oprah Winfrey Show*. This gave Oprah complete control over her talk show. She became the first African-American woman to own a television or film-production company, and she was the third woman ever to do so. The other two were Mary Pickford and Lucille Ball.

By 1991, Oprah was making $80 million a year. She was ranked the third-richest entertainer in the world. Because of her financial success, she has been able to concentrate on producing films and television programs that are meaningful to her. Oprah wanted to bring social issues into the public's eye so, in 1988, she produced a mini-series called *The Women of Brewster Place*. It was about the lives of a group of women living in a **ghetto**. In 1998, Oprah produced and starred in a film based on Toni Morrison's *Beloved*, the award-winning book about slavery.

Oprah has started many scholarship programs for students in university. She personally watches their progress and sends them letters of encouragement.

Quick Notes

- Oprah knew how to read by the time she was two and a half years old.

- Harpo, the name of Oprah's television and film-production company, is Oprah spelled backwards.

- Oprah's mother named her Orpah, but it was misspelled on her birth certificate.

- Oprah is a part-owner in three television stations and a restaurant.

- "The Queen of Talk" is the nickname the media has given Oprah.

Oprah is the national spokesperson for an organization called A Better Chance. It provides scholarships to inner-city students to go to the best schools in the United States.

"Someone has to show you the light in order to survive, the light of love, and I truly don't know who showed me mine. Except, perhaps God. I always felt He was there."

More Women in Profile

The following pages list a few more women entrepreneurs you may want to read about on your own. Use the Suggested Reading list to learn about these and other women entrepreneurs.

Princess Shahnaz Husain

1938–
Giuliana Benetton
Cofounder of Benetton Group

Born in Italy, Giuliana started knitting sweaters at the age of thirteen to help support the family after her father died. Her brother sold her colorful creations to local stores, delivering them by bicycle. Their business grew over the years to include more products, such as watches, jewelry, and perfume. Between 1983 and 1986, the family-run Benetton Group opened clothing stores all over the world at a rate of one per day. Today, Benetton is Europe's largest clothing manufacturer.

1926–
Ernestina Laura Herrera De Noble
President of Grupo Clarin

Argentina's Ernestina owns and directs the newspaper *Diario Clarin*, which sells more copies than any other Spanish-language newspaper in the world. Because it is an independent newspaper, *Diario Clarin* acts as a watchdog on the government. Ernestina strongly believes in freedom of the press and encourages her editors to print the truth about government officials and policies.

1942–
Princess Shahnaz Husain
Founder of Shahnaz Herbals

Shahnaz was horrified when she traveled outside India and saw the unnatural ingredients used in **cosmetics** in the western world. She decided to begin a business, using flowers and herbs, to make cosmetics. Her company, Shahnaz Herbals, makes products including toothpaste, acne cream, pain killers, and lipstick. Shahnaz makes products for different ages, sexes, and races, and also for animals. Shahnaz was the first person honored with the World's Greatest Woman Entrepreneur Award given by *America's Success* magazine in 1996.

1923–

Jean Nidetch

Founder of Weight Watchers International

Since her childhood in Brooklyn, New York, Jean thought of herself as overweight. She tried many different diets, and in 1961, she at last found one that worked. To stay on the diet, she got together with six friends who had the same goal. The group talked about their efforts at losing weight. Jean and her friends found this support more helpful than anything they had tried in the past. They shared the cost of buying a scale and checked their weight every week. Gradually, more and more people came, and Jean founded Weight Watchers International. The company's program of **nutrition**, moderation, and sharing experiences became so popular that people from around the world began opening up **franchises**. Since then, thirty-two million people around the world have joined Weight Watchers.

1872–1943

Omu Okwei

Market Queen

Omu Okwei was born into a wealthy family of merchants in Ossomari, an important trading town in Eastern Nigeria. Despite her family's wealth, she started her business with no money because only Nigerian men inherited land or money from their parents. Omu started trading fruit and vegetables but quickly switched to imported goods, such as lamps, pots, beads, and gunpowder. Her business prospered, and she gained a reputation as the most important female merchant in the area. In 1935, Okwei was given the title Omu of Ossomari ("Queen of Ossomari"). Her duties included advising the king in making decisions on behalf of the town, running the local market, and settling disputes among the town's citizens.

Jean Nidetch

1921–

Chanut Piyaoui

Founder of Dusit Thani Public Company Limited

While visiting New York City, Chanut decided that she wanted to build a grand hotel, like the ones she saw in America, at home in Thailand. After several years of raising money, which included selling her own jewelry, she opened her first hotel. She called it The Princess. It was the first hotel in Thailand with a swimming pool. In 1969, Chanut built Bangkok's first high-rise hotel, the Dusit Thani, which means "Town in Heaven." She now owns more than sixty hotels in seventeen countries. The King of Thailand honored Chanut with the title Khunying for her work in promoting Thailand's tourism.

1955–

Emilia Roxas

Chairperson of Asiaworld Internationale

Determination is what got Emilia to the position of chairperson of her family's Taiwan-based company. It is a world-wide organization with a range of businesses that include banks, hotels, resorts, and manufacturing and publishing companies. Born and raised in the Philippines, Emilia started working in the family business at age ten, doing odd jobs. By the time she was thirty-three, she was running the company.

1897–1967

Margaret Fogarty Rudkin

Founder of Pepperidge Farm

Born in New York City, Margaret did not bake her first loaf of bread until she was almost forty years old. She started baking because her doctor said that her son needed food made from natural ingredients to help his asthma. After several unsuccessful attempts, Margaret made a nutritious and tasty loaf of bread. It was so good that she was soon selling it to her doctor, his patients, and local grocery stores. As her business grew, she moved her bakery into her garage, and then into her stables. Her products, which she called Pepperidge Farm, became more and more popular. When she sold the company in 1960, its yearly sales had reached $32 million.

Margaret Forgarty Rudkin

1867–1919

Madame C.J. Walker

Founder of Mme C.J. Walker's Preparations

Madame C.J. Walker was the first African-American woman to make a million dollars. She made her fortune by identifying a problem, inventing a cure for it, and selling that cure. In those days, many African Americans tried to straighten their hair by twisting it and wrapping it with string. This caused hair loss. Madame C.J. Walker invented Wonderful Hair Grower, which not only stopped hair falling out, but caused it to grow back. She started her business with only one dollar and fifty cents. By the time she died, there were more than 25,000 women selling her products.

1940–

Nina Wang

Chairperson of Chinachem Group

Nina has one of the tallest buildings in the world named after her. It is the 108-story Nina Tower in Hong Kong. Nina paid for the entire construction with cash. She is thought to be Asia's richest woman and the second-richest woman in the world. Nina's road to success has had its hardships. She and her husband were joint directors of the Chinachem Group, which buys, develops, and sells property. In 1983, Nina's husband was kidnapped, and Nina paid $11 million for his release. In 1990, he was kidnapped again. Although Nina paid the kidnappers $30 million, she never saw her husband again. Now, Nina alone controls the Chinachem Group and is highly respected in the business world.

1865–1950

Elsie de Wolfe

Interior Designer

The daughter of a Canadian doctor, Elsie had a talent for decorating houses. After settling in New York City, she began decorating her friends' homes. Soon, she decided to become a professional interior designer. Elsie became known as the "Founding Mother" of the decorating profession.

Elsie de Wolfe

Glossary

astride: with one leg on each side

cerebral palsy: a disability caused by damage to the brain before birth

cleft palate: when the roof of the mouth is not joined together

competitor: a person who takes part in something in the hope of doing better than others

cosmetics: products used to beautify the face or some other part of the body

couturier: a fashion designer

covet: to want something that belongs to someone else

designs: sketches or patterns from which clothing is made

exclusive: only for select people

franchises: people or shops that have the right to sell a company's goods

ghetto: a crowded, low-income area of a city

Greenpeace: an organization that tries to protect the environment

heirloom: a valued family possession

merchandising: selling

negotiate: arrange the terms of

news anchor: a reporter who reads the news

nobility: people of high rank or status, such as counts and dukes

nutrition: nourishing food

pharmacology: the science of drugs

physiology: the study of living things, their parts, and their functions

potpourri: a mixture of dried flower petals, spices, and herbs

professional: making money from doing something

recession: a period when earnings and employment are below normal levels

retailing: selling goods directly to customers

seamstress: a woman who sews

Suggested Reading

Bielow, Barbara Carlisle. *Contemporary Black Biography*. Volume 2. Detroit: Gale Research, 1992.

Fucini, Joseph J., and Suzy Fucini. *Entrepreneurs: The Men and Women behind Famous Brand Names and How They Made It*. Boston: G.K. Hall., 1985.

Rediger, Pat. *Great African Americans in Business*. Niagara-on-the-Lake: Crabtree Publishing Company, 1996.

Roddick, Anita. *Body and Soul*. London: Ebury Press, 1991.

Saari, Peggy. *Prominent Women of the 20th Century*. Detroit: UXL, 1986.

Silver, A. David. *Enterprising Women*. New York: AMACOM, 1994.

Smith, Jessie Carney, ed. *Notable Black American Women*. Detroit: Gale Research, 1992.

Straub, Deborah Gillan, ed. *Contemporary Heroes and Heroines*. Detroit: Gale Research, 1992.

Index

1 2 3 4 5 6 7 8 9 0 Printed in Canada 8 7 6 5 4 3 2 1 0 9